Snake Cake

by Pearl Markovics

Consultant:
Beth Gambro
Reading Specialist
Yorkville, Illinois

Contents

BEARPORT
PUBLISHING

New York, New York

Snake Cake

Let's rhyme!

This is **Jake**.

He lives on a **lake**.

Jake loves to **bake**.

He makes a big, tasty **cake**.

Here is **Jake's** pet **snake**.

The hungry **snake** is **awake**.

The **snake** wants some **cake**.

"Oh no!" says **Jake**.

Key Words in the -ake Family

awake

bake

cake

lake

snake

Other **-ake** Words:
brake, fake, stake, take

Index

About the Author

Pearl Markovics enjoys having fun with words. She especially likes witty wordplay.